Bradwell's

ECLECTICA ®

A FEAST OF FUN, FACTS AND HISTORY!

HAMPSHIRE

GW00702924

Published by Bradwell Books
9 Orgreave Close Sheffield S13 9NP
Email: books@bradwellbooks.co.uk

Bradwell's Eclectica is a registered trade mark
of NMD Trading, Sheffield. UK.
® Number. UK 00003048225

1st Edition

ISBN: 9781909914599

Design by: Andrew Caffrey

Print: Gutenberg Press, Malta

Photograph Credits: Shutterstock, iStock, Creative
Commons and credited individually. All other
images are © the author.

Cover Image: iSTOCK

Mapping: Ordnance Survey Mapping used under
licence from the Ordnance Survey.

Ordnance Survey Partner Number100039353

Acknowledgements

Thanks go to my partner, Tony, for his enthusiasm
and unflagging willingness to jump in the car with
his camera, at the drop of a hat, and drive us off to
some far-flung corner of Hampshire for research
and photography!

Thanks also to Tim Horne for the Typhoon
photograph taken at Farnborough Airshow, and
to John Elder who, when I found out he lived in
Selborne, willingly agreed to take photographs
of Gilbert White's house and gardens, where he
volunteers with his wife in the museum.

And finally thanks to Chris Gilbert of Bradwell Books,
who seems not to be offended when I answer his
progress-checking phone calls with a 'Go away'!

Bradwell's

ECLECTICA

A FEAST OF FUN, FACTS AND HISTORY!

HAMPSHIRE

Linda Fernley

BRADWELL
BOOKS

Contents

WALKS

Two short but informative walks around Winchester will provide a deeper insight into this highly attractive and ancient city.

LOCAL EVENTS

Find out about some of the things that make Hampshire special, and that bring visitors back year after year.

LOCAL HISTORY

So much to say and so little space... a smattering of Hampshire's history to whet your appetite to dig a bit deeper!

GHOST STORIES

If you like to be spooked out, then these ghost stories will do the trick. If headless ladies and green men aren't your cup of tea, skip this section!

LOCAL SPORTS

Hampshire is the home of English cricket, but there's lots more going on besides that. Find out what.

FAMOUS LOCALS

Authors, actors, and artists; scientists and designers; prime ministers and TV gardeners; sports presenters and French emperors! What a truly eclectic bunch of 'locals'!

INTRODUCTION

HAMPSHIRE, THE LARGEST COUNTY IN SOUTH-EAST ENGLAND AND THE THIRD LARGEST UK 'SHIRE', HAS A HUGE AMOUNT TO OFFER.

Unspoilt scenery, rivers and coasts, beautiful country houses, attractive villages and interesting market towns. Despite a large number of populated towns and cities, a huge 45 per cent of Hampshire is taken up with two National Parks – the South Downs and the unique New Forest. And then there's the Isle of Wight; although no longer administratively part of

Isle of Wight iStock

Hampshire, it's only half an hour by ferry from the mainland, and people still associate it with the county. It's only 23 miles by 13 miles but boasts the world-famous Round the Island Boat Race, the family home of Queen Victoria, and the renowned Isle of Wight Music Festival, all of which attract thousands of visitors each year.

Hampshire is the birthplace of all three of the British Forces: the Army still resides in Aldershot; the RAF began life in Farnborough, my home town and one which still plays an important part in UK aviation; and the coastal towns of Portsmouth and Southampton have strong links with the Royal Navy.

Hampshire's county town, Winchester, was historically the capital of England, and is still home to the largest medieval cathedral in Europe.

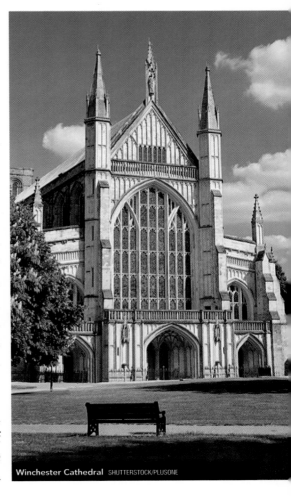

Winchester Cathedral SHUTTERSTOCK/PLUSONE

Portsmouth iSTOCK

Southampton and Portsmouth are both large, bustling and vibrant port cities, steeped in nautical history and awash (pardon the pun!) with commercial progress and cultural heritage. Southampton handles a large proportion of the UK's national container freight while Portsmouth is home to a huge Royal Navy base. Inland, Basingstoke, often mistaken for a new town, is in fact an old market town expanded in the 1960s in order to accommodate part of the London 'overspill'. Basingstoke market was mentioned in the Domesday Book of 1086; it still has a regular market,

it's a county that never fails to inspire. From historic docks and modern marinas on the Solent coast, to the leafy New Forest National Park packed full of lovely wild ponies, donkeys, and even pigs, the variety is endless.

The Anvil, Basingstoke

but is now a large and important economic business centre. Hampshire has more than its fair share of famous authors – Dickens, Austen, and Conan Doyle to name a few; it has nautical cities with old-age naval war ships, sail-shaped towers and resurrected Tudor merchant vessels;

It's the home of English cricket, hosts one of the world's largest international air shows, and you'll find the National Motor Museum and the largest UK watercress growing region in the

New Forest Ponies iStock

south, the latter of which inspired the quintessentially British steam train route – the Watercress Line. And Hampshire also represents the end of the line for the Napoleon dynasty! The county's museums are packed with armour, military paraphernalia and submarines. You can discover the Round Table of Arthurian legend, or buy a yacht at the UK's biggest boat show! However, if what you're looking for is little bit of factual information interspersed with a light-hearted overview of some of Hampshire's peculiarities, then this is the book for you. You can read about some of its notorious murders and chilling ghost stories, or try your hand at some of its tasty – and unusual –

recipes. Or, if you're after silly jokes or local customs, or want to know about its famous people, then you can do that here, too.

With a county so large, so rich in heritage, and with such a variety of landscapes, towns, and villages, I can do no more with a book of this size than simply scratch the surface of Hampshire's character. However, I hope that in so doing, I've given you enough to whet your appetite to find out more for yourselves. I've lived in or near to the county for several decades, and its people and places never fail to rouse my curiosity; there's always another surprise just around the corner!

LOCAL DIALECT

THERE'S A GENERAL BELIEF THAT HAMPSHIRE IS A 'POSH' COUNTY, WHOSE INHABITANTS SPEAK IN A 'QUEEN'S ENGLISH' ACCENT.

However, in my experience, use of 'Estuary' English – a halfway-house between cockney and standard English – is more common and, also contrary to popular belief, very few people in Hampshire use a west country 'oo arr' accent or dialect!

Hampshire Hog (or 'ampshire 'og) was used in jest to describe a Hampshire person, the county being famous for 'a fine breed of hogs, and the excellency of the bacon made there'! CREATIVE COMMONS

In the early 19th century, people living in rural south-west Hampshire, particularly the New Forest, spoke a dialect which is now rarely heard. You can still find traces of words peculiar to the area, and the accent itself has changed little, but nowadays you're not likely to hear someone ask, *'Wair did ur cum vrom?'* ('Where did she come from?'), *'Bist dhee gwein too?'* ('Are you going, too?') or *'Haih, loo see, dhaier's a scuggee muggings zittin on t' gaalay-baagur!'* (Look, see, there's a squirrel sitting on the scarecrow')!

Sadly, along with many other local dialects around the British Isles, the use of a Hampshire dialect has steadily decreased as the population has became more mobile over the past

75 years. So the following glossary is a selection of words taken from what older local Hampshire people either remember or still use, and from a collection of New Forester's dialect recorded mainly at the turn of the last century.

A

Aaf – off
Aan't – haven't
Aarchurd – orchard
Aardinury – ordinary
Aarkurd – awkward
Addur – after
Aess – to ask, asked
Affeared – afraid
Afoar – before
Agg – egg
Ait – eat
Aul – all
Avroze – frozen, icy (of weather or conditions)

B

Baavin – bundle of small boughs
Baggur – beggar
Baich – beech
Baint – aren't, isn't
Bair – beer
Baird – beard
Baist – beast
Barn – born
Baug – bog
Blaakay – blackbird
Blather – a fuss, uproar
Blood-turnip – beetroot
Bottom – hollow, low-lying land
Butturvloi – butterfly

C

Caarn – corn, wheat
Cackleberry – egg
Caddle – muddle
Chandler – a dealer in soap and candles
Chawbacon – an unsophisticated person; a bumpkin or yokel

Chiffay – chaffinch
Chinkay – chaffinch
Chiselbob – woodlouse
Chock – block of wood
Clot – turf
Clum – handle clumsily
Cooud – cold

D

Daartur – daughter
Dhay – they, those, these
Dheezelf – yourself
Dhem – them, those
Dhenk – think
Dhurzelvz – themselves
Diddee/diddeecay – gypsy
Dimmet, dimpsey – dusk
Drang – a narrow lane or alleyway between buildings
Dreckly – directly, straight away
Dus'n – doesn't

E

Ee – he
Eef – if

Eer – hear
Eerd – heard
Ees – yes
Ei – I
Em – them
Enny wen – at any time
Extray – extra

F

Faarist – forest
Faivur – fever
Feesh – fish
Figgety pudden – plum-pudding, the forerunner of Christmas pudding
Foar-haars – leading horse in a team
Fust – first

G

Gaalay-baagur (or gallibagger) – scarecrow
Gaffer (and granfer) – grandfather
Gakeing – daydreaming
Gawermush – policeman
Gee, gi – give
Gel – girl

Gerdin – garden
Gi – give
Girt – great, big, large
Goosegogs – gooseberries
Gowk – cuckoo
Grammer – grandmother
Gurt – great, as in big
Gwein – part, going

H

Haars, has – horse, pony
Haast – has
Haih! – eh! what!
Hef – half
Heidee-hoop – hide-and-seek
Heil – bundle of wheat
Hervist – harvest
Hid – head
Hizzelf – himself
Hob – potato-pit
Hoss, has – horse

I

Id – head
Idhout – outside

Id'n – isn't
Irrjin – engine

J

Jillay staak – gilliflower (type of carnation)
Joaay – a threepenny bit
Job – difficulty
Joppety-joppety – in a state of nervous anxiety, jittery

K

Kent – can't
Kiddil – kettle
Kist – an ancient burial mound
Kiwur – cover
Kushti – good

L

Laang – long
Leat – a stream
Leeray – empty (usually referring to hunger)
Limber – slim or slender (of a person)

Loo see – look you
Low – allow, think, dare say

M

Maarnin – morning
Maistur – master
Mallyshag – caterpillar
Mast – beech-nuts and acorns
Mauz – heap of corn in the straw
Meind – remember
Mezelf – myself
Mid – might
Mid be – maybe
Mid'n – might not
Moak – donkey
Moast – very
Mommet – a scarecrow
Mooustly – generally
Muss – must
Muss'n – must not

N

Naarth – north
Naut – nothing
Nestay – nasty

Niwur – never
Noad – knew, known
Noo – no
Numshon – luncheon
Nus – nurse

O

Oa – of
Offin – often
Oi – I, and yes
Oss – horse
Oun – hound
Ourn – ours

P

Paakit – pocket
Pag – peg
Paipul – people
Palmer – caterpillar
Pay – pea
Pecty – covered with little spots of decay
Pinchfart – mean, tight
Plaiz – please
Pook – heap of hay

Pyooit – lapwing

Q

Quag – bog or marshy area
Qwair – queer
Qweiut – quiet
Qwid – cud

R

Rail – real
Raip – reap
Randy – rustic celebration, often for a wedding or harvest
Rayed – dressed
Reit – right, thoroughly, quite
Rick – stack
Ruff – roof

S

Saart – sort
Scuggee muggings – squirrel
Seed – seen
Shaart – short
Shrammed – frozen or cold to the bone

Slug-abed – sluggard, lazy person
Sowbugs – woodlice
Spaik – speak
Spek – expect
Spoaz – suppose
Staarm – storm
Stabble – to walk about aimlessly
Stray – straw
Strickle – block upon which a blade, usually a scythe or sickle, was sharpened
Stroy – destroy, kill off
Summat – something
Swait – sweet

T

T' – the
Taarbul – terribly
Taarmint – torment
Taffety – fanciful
Taichur – teacher
Taitay – potato
Tedn't – it isn't
Tiddee – potato
'Tiddin, 'tiddn't – isn't

Tiz – it is
Toad – told
T'odher – the other
Tremenjus – tremendous
Tut-work – piece-work, paid for by the number of units produced
Twoald – tell, told

U

Un – him
Unrayed – undressed
Ur – her, them, or

V

Vaalur – value
Vaarist – forest
Vaark – fork
Vaarm – warm
Vaarmur – warmer
Vaartneit – fortnight
Veeld – field
Vinggur – finger
Vittles – food, provisions or ingredients
Vloi – fly

Vorgit – forget
Voul – fowl
Vound – found
Vur – for, or fir
Vurdher – further off
Vurdhist – furthest
Vurray – very

W

Waak – walk
Waar – war
Waark – work
Warm – worm
Weeout – without
Wer – was, were
Werret – to worry or a worry
Widhee – willow
Wik – week
Wind-list – white streak of faint cloud across a clear blue sky
Wint – went
Withywind – climbing plant also known as bindweed
Wit'n – will not
Woak – oak

Woald – old
Woald-faashun – old-fashioned
Wood'n – wouldn't
Woots – would
Wops – wasp
Wot – who, which, what, that
Woz'n (and wozzint) – wasn't
Wuirk – work
Wust – worst
Wuts – oats

Y

Yaalur – yellow
Yaandur – yonder
Yaaprun – apron
Yaas – yes
Yaeker – acorn
Yaffle – green woodpecker
Yeer – here, and ear
Yoa – ewe
Yoorn – yours
Yungin – young one, youngster

Z

Zay – sea, say

Zayin – saying
Zbeidur – spider
Zeid – side
Zeit – sight
Zelf – self
Zet – sat, sit
Zich – such
Zid, zeed – saw, seen
Zizurz – scissors
Zoa – sow
Zoid – side
Zoidur – cider
Zoo – so
Zouth – south
Zow – sow
Zummit – something

HUMOUR

SIDE-SPLITTING JOKES FROM HILARIOUS HAMPSHIRE!

Simon was down on his luck so he thought he would try getting a few odd jobs by calling at the posh houses in Brockenhurst. After a few 'no ways', a guy in one of the big houses thought he would give him a break and says, 'The porch needs painting so I'll give you £50 to paint it for me.'

'You're a life-saver, mister,' says Simon. 'I'll get started right away!'

Time passes until . . .

'There you go, I'm all done with the painting.'

'Well, here's your £50,' says the homeowner, handing over some crisp tenners.

'Thanks very much,' says Simon, pocketing the money. 'Oh and by the way, it's a Ferrari, not a Porsche!'

Two rival cricketers from Petersfield and Waterlooville were having a chat.

'The local team wants me to play for them very badly,' said the man from Waterlooville.

'Well,' said his friend, 'you're just the man for the job.'

A rather cocky young man, who worked on a busy construction site in Portsmouth, was bragging that he could outdo anyone in a feat of strength. He made a special case of making fun of Morris, one of the more senior workmen. After several minutes, Morris had had enough.

'Why don't you put your money where your mouth is?' he said. 'I'll bet a week's wages that I can haul something in a wheelbarrow over to that outbuilding that you won't be able to wheel back again.'

'You're on, mate,' the cocky young man replied. 'It's a bet! Let's see what you got.'

Morris reached out and grabbed the wheelbarrow by the handles. Then, nodding to the young man, he said, 'All right. Get in.'

TOB

A couple from the Isle of Wight had been courting for nearly twenty years. One day as they sat on a seat in the park, the woman plucked up the courage to ask:

'Don't you think it's time we got married?'
Her sweetheart answered:
'Yes, but who'd have us?'

....

Two ladies were enjoying a latte in their Bramshott coffee shop. One said to the other, 'Was it love at first sight when you met your husband?'

'No, I don't think so,' came the reply. 'I didn't know how much money he had when I first met him!'

....

Derek and Duncan were long-time neighbours in Ringwood. Every time Derek saw Duncan coming round to his house, his heart sank. This was because he knew that, as always, Duncan would be visiting him in order to borrow something, and he was fed up with it.

'I'm not going to let Duncan get away with it this time,' he said quietly to his wife. 'Watch what I'm about to do.'

'Hi there, I wondered if you were

thinking about using your hedge trimmer this afternoon?' asked Duncan.

'Oh, I'm very sorry,' said Derek, trying to look apologetic, 'but I'm actually going to be using it all afternoon.'

'In that case,' replied Duncan with a big grin, 'you won't be using your golf clubs, will you? Mind if I borrow them?'

....

A well-known Portsmouth academic was giving a lecture on the philosophy of language at the University. He came to a curious aspect of English grammar.

'You will note,' said the somewhat stuffy scholar, 'that in the English language, two negatives can mean a positive, but it is never the case that two positives can mean a negative.'

To which someone at the back responded, 'Yeah, yeah.'

....

A reporter from the Hampshire Chronicle was covering the local football league and went to see Liss Athetic FC versus Liphook United. One of the Liss players looked so old he went over to him and said, 'You know, you might be the oldest man playing in the league. How do you do it at your age?'

The man replied, 'I drink six pints every night, smoke two packets of fags a day, and eat tons of chips.'

'Wow, that is incredible!' said the reporter. 'How old did you say you were?'

'Twenty-two,' said the player proudly.

....

A farmer was driving along a country road near the village of Chilbolton with a large load of fertiliser. A little boy, playing in front of his house, saw him and called out, 'What do you have on your truck?'

'Fertiliser,' the farmer replied.

'What are you going to do with it?' asked the little boy.

'Put it on strawberries,' answered the farmer.

'You ought to live here,' the little boy

advised him. 'We put sugar and cream on ours.'

....

A woman got on a bus in Basingstoke but soon regretted it. The driver sped down the high street, zigzagging across the lanes, breaking nearly every rule of the road. Unable to take it any longer, the woman stepped forward, her voice shaking as she spoke. 'You're a shocking driver! I am so afraid of sitting on your bus, I don't know what to do.'

'Do what I do,' said the bus driver. 'Close your eyes!'

....

An Alton couple, Enid and Sidney, are having matrimonial difficulties and seek the advice of a counsellor. The couple are shown into a room where the counsellor asks Enid what problems, in her opinion, she faces in her relationship with Sidney.

'Well,' she starts, 'he shows me no affection. I don't seem to be important to him any more. We don't share the same interests and I don't think he loves me at all.' Enid has tears in her eyes as the counsellor walks over to her, gives her a big hug and kisses her firmly on the lips.

Sidney looks on in passive disbelief. The counsellor turns to Sidney and says, 'This is what Enid needs once a day for the next month. Can you see that she gets it?'

Sidney looks unsettled. 'Well, I can drop her off every day other than Wednesdays when I play snooker and Sundays when I go fishing!'

....

'You're looking glum,' the captain of Andover Cricket Club remarked to one of his players.

'Yes, the doctor says I can't play cricket,' said the downcast man.

'Really?' replied the captain. 'I didn't know he'd ever seen you play?'

RECIPES

TASTY DISHES FROM AROUND HAMPSHIRE!

Hampshire Haslet

Haslet comes from the old French word for entrails, but don't worry – it now just refers to the fact that all the ingredients are very finely minced!

iStock

See **page 28** for recipe

Watercress Soup

iStock

INGREDIENTS:

15ml/1 tbsp olive oil

1 small onion, chopped

1 small stick celery

350g potato, peeled and diced

600ml chicken or vegetable stock

3 (85g) bags watercress

150ml milk

Pinch of nutmeg

Squeeze of lemon juice

Salt and freshly ground black pepper

PREPARATION:

1. Heat oil in large pan, add onion and celery and sauté over medium heat for **5 minutes** until pale golden.

2. Stir in potato and stock and bring to the boil. Cover and simmer for **10 minutes** or until the potato is tender.

3. Stir in watercress, cover and cook for a further **5 minutes** or until watercress is wilted.

4. Transfer soup to a food processor and blitz until smooth.

5. Return soup to the rinsed-out pan, add milk, nutmeg, lemon juice and seasoning to taste.

6. Gently reheat until piping hot and serve with crusty bread.

Hampshire Friar's Omelette JOAN RANSLEY

I couldn't get to the bottom of why this was specifically called a 'Hampshire' Friar's omelette but was intrigued enough to try it; gosh, those Hampshire Friars had a good palette - *yummy!*

INGREDIENTS:

4 good-sized cooking apples

50gm sugar

Grated rind and flesh of 1 lemon

4 tablespoons breadcrumbs

85g butter

4 egg yolks

Cloves or nutmeg to flavour

PREPARATION:

1. Peel, core and slice apples, stew in a little water until soft. Allow to cool.

2. Cream butter and sugar together until light and fluffy.

3. Add chopped flesh and rind of lemon together with grated cloves or nutmeg to the creamed butter and sugar mix.

4. Grease a pie dish and sprinkle with about one tablespoon of breadcrumbs.

5. Beat yolks into the stewed apple in the saucepan.

6. Pour the apple into the pie dish. Dot the creamed butter mixture over the apples, cover with remaining breadcrumbs, and finish with small pats of butter on top.

7. Bake in a moderate oven at 160°C for 1½ hours until the breadcrumbs are golden and the apples have set to a custard like consistency.

Hampshire Haslet

INGREDIENTS:

450g pork shoulder

1 medium cooking onion, quartered

150g breadcrumbs

1 to **1½** teaspoons chopped sage

¼ teaspoon hot red chilli

Salt and pepper to taste

Melted pork lard for greasing

PREPARATION:

1. Mince half the pork into a bowl, then the onion, then the rest of the pork (this ensures all the onion gets through the mince). Add all other ingredients (except for lard) and mix well.

2. Preheat oven to 170°C / Gas 3.

3. Take a 1lb loaf tin, grease well with lard, or line with baking paper and lightly grease.

4. Put the mix into the tin, ensuring no gaps are left in the corners.

5. Place into oven, bake for 1½ to 2 hours or until the centre is hot.

6. Take out of oven and allow to cool. Slice fairly thinly and enjoy!

TIP

Check halfway through cooking; if the top is browning too quickly, loosely cover with foil.

MURDERS

TERRIBLE TIMES ON THE STREETS OF HAMPSHIRE

THE GRUESOME MURDER OF SWEET FANNY ADAMS

You've most likely heard of the expression **'Sweet Fanny Adams'** but do you know its origin? When the name Fanny Adams made the headlines in 1867, it sent a shockwave of revulsion and sadness around the country; she was brutally murdered on Saturday 24 August of that year in Alton.

Fanny and her friend, Minnie Warner, both eight years old, set off up the lane with Fanny's seven-year-old sister, Lizzie. A respectable looking man, wearing a black frock coat, waistcoat and trousers approached them. He offered Minnie three halfpence to go off and spend with Lizzie, while Fanny could have a halfpenny if she alone would go with him up The Hollow, an old road leading to the nearby village of Shalden. Fanny took her halfpenny but refused to go with him, so he picked her up and carried her into a nearby hopfield, out of sight of the other children. It was then almost 1.30pm.

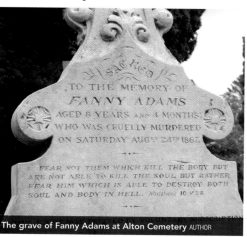

The grave of Fanny Adams at Alton Cemetery AUTHOR

At about five o'clock, having played together since Fanny was taken by the man, Minnie and Lizzie went home. Realising Fanny was missing, her anxious mother and a neighbour hurried up the lane, where they met the same man coming from the direction of The Hollow.

When they questioned him, he said he often gave money to children and that Fanny had left unharmed to rejoin the others. Because he appeared respectable and told them he was a clerk of a local solicitor, they let him leave.

At seven o'clock Fanny was still missing, so worried neighbours formed a search party, who found poor Fanny's body in the field.

The obvious suspect was arrested that evening at his workplace in Alton High Street. 'I know nothing about it,' said 29-year-old Frederick Baker as he was taken through an angry crowd to Alton Police Station. Baker's shirt and trousers were found to be spotted with blood. His boots, socks and trouser bottoms were wet. Two small knives, one stained with blood, were discovered when he was searched. Witnesses confirmed he'd been away from the solicitor's office between 1pm and 3.25pm, and then went out again until 5.30pm. Mrs Adams had seen him coming from the direction of the hopfield some time after 5pm: if, as seems likely, he had murdered Fanny Adams during his first absence, had he then returned to commit further atrocities?

On the following Monday, while searching Baker's office desk, the police found his diary; shortly before his arrest he'd written: '24th August, Saturday – killed a young girl. It was fine and hot.'

A local painter also found a large

stone in the hopfield covered with blood, hair and a piece of flesh. This was pronounced as the probable murder weapon; the post-mortem found death had been caused by a fatal blow to Fanny's head.

Baker's trial opened at Winchester Assizes on 5 December. Minnie Warner was made to testify; the defence challenged her identification of Baker and claimed that it was impossible for his small knives to have dismembered Fanny so thoroughly. The defence's case focused on Baker's state of mind, a sorry story of genetic insanity. His father had 'shown an inclination to assault, even to kill, his children'; a cousin had been in asylums four times; brain fever had caused his sister's death; and he had attempted suicide after an abortive love affair.

Unimpressed, the jury rejected the judge's advice that they might consider the prisoner not guilty due to insanity (a plea often heard in our courts today). However, after only 15 minutes the jury returned a guilty verdict, and Baker was hanged before a crowd of 5,000 in front of Winchester's County Prison at 8am on Christmas Eve, 1867.

Baker was hanged on Christmas Eve, 1867
CREATIVE COMMONS

AN UNSOLVED CASE OF STRYCHNINE POISONING

Hubert George Chevis (1902–31), a lieutenant in the Royal Artillery of the British Army, was the victim of an unsolved murder in June 1931. He died of poisoning after eating contaminated partridge.

The son of Sir William and Lady Amy

Florence Chevis, Hubert was born at Rawalpindi in India, where he spent his school years, and later attended Charterhouse School in Surrey. He graduated from the Royal Military Academy as a Second Lieutenant in 1923. At the time of his death in 1931 Chevis was an instructor at the Aldershot Training Camp in Hampshire, and had been married for six months to Frances, a 29-year-old heiress with considerable wealth. Chevis was her second husband, the first having been Major George Jackson, a vet.

On the afternoon of 20 June 1931 the couple had friends over for cocktails at their Blackdown Camp home. When the friends had gone, the couple had an early dinner, as they were planning to attend the local military tattoo that evening. Dinner, a partridge, had been prepared by their cook, carved by Frances Chevis, and served by their batman, Gunner Nicholas Bulger. After Chevis had eaten a mouthful of the bird, he summoned Bulger to take the bird away, claiming it was 'the most terrible thing I have tasted'. Mrs Chevis also tasted the meat and agreed. The partridges were incinerated in the kitchen by the cook. Shortly after eating

The poisoner was never discovered! iStock

the mouthful of partridge, Chevis experienced severe cramps and convulsions, and a doctor was called. Later that evening, Mrs Chevis also fell ill. A second doctor came and they were both admitted to Frimley Cottage Hospital. Chevis died at 1am the following morning; two grains of strychnine were found in his stomach.

Anyone for partridge?! CREATIVE COMMONS

Mrs Chevis subsequently recovered, as she had barely tasted the meat.

Chevis's death was reported in The Times on 22 June. Two days later, on the day of the funeral, his father Sir William Chevis received a telegram from a J. Hartigan, sent from Dublin. All it said was: 'Hooray, hooray, hooray!' The telegram was labelled with the name of the 'Hibernian', a well-known hotel in Dublin. The police were notified, but nobody of that name was found at the hotel. Later enquiries by the Dublin Police found that a chemist in the city had sold strychnine about four weeks earlier to a man similar in appearance to the man who'd sent the telegram from the post office.

Many theories were put forward about the death, but the investigation stalled because of a lack of evidence. An open verdict was returned.

The case was the subject of a BBC Radio 4 documentary in 2011. Again, due to lack of evidence, the programme was unable to reach any firm conclusions, but noted that none of the initial suspects (presumably the cook, the butler and the wife) had both motive and opportunity. It also pointed out that both Chevis and his father had strong connections to the British Raj, and that 'J Hartigan' is an anagram of 'Raj hating'. **What do you think?!**

iSTOCK

SHOT FOR GIVING ORDERS!

In July 1869, Corporal James Brett of the 2nd Battalion 7th Royal Fusiliers, based at Aldershot, was in charge of a regiment of soldiers tasked with emptying and refilling beds in the barrack stores. One of his men, Private William Dixon, was told to fill some extra beds but refused, saying that he'd already done his fair share. Corporal Brett went to report his behaviour to his superiors, and when he returned Dixon shot and killed him with his rifle. The bullet went right through his head and out of the window, narrowly missing some ladies in the married quarters next door!

Dixon had a reputation for being aggressive and disobedient, and had already been in trouble for previous offences. At his trial he claimed that Brett continually bullied him, but he was sentenced to death and hanged on 6 September.

LOCAL NAMES

THERE ARE ABOUT 300 PLACE NAMES IN HAMPSHIRE, WHOSE ORIGINS CONTAIN A WEALTH OF HISTORY AND ROMANCE.

All are worth exploring, but that would take another book! So here are just a few. In the middle of Hampshire is the village of **Micheldever** on the River Dever. In the 9th century the name was recorded as Mycendefr. Linguists think it's a Celtic name and the meaning appears to be **'boggy waters'**. The second part of the name, **defr**, means 'stream'. So **River Dever** means **River River!** That's not unusual, though; the Avon and Ouse are also old Britannic words meaning 'river', so the **River Avon** is also the **River River,** as

Woodland at Micheldever SHUTTERSTOCK/ RTIMAGES

Bridge at Basingstoke

is the River **Ouse.** To the north of the county is Basingstoke, made up of three Old English elements: **Basa + inga + stoc. Basa** is the name of a Saxon leader. **Inga** means possession of a place by the people led by the named person. **Stoc** means 'outlying farmstead'. Putting all these together, Basingstoke means the place where you'll find the isolated farm owned by the people once led by Basa! JOHN ARLOTT, the famous voice of cricket, with a much-loved **'Hampshire burr'**, called his autobiography Basingstoke Boy, because he was brought up in the then pretty market town in the early 20th century.

And what about Winchester, the city at the centre of the county and its history? The Romans named the settlement they found there **Venta Belgarum,** meaning **'Chief Place of the Belgae'.** **Belgae** was what the Romans called Britons living in the area now called Hampshire, having previously met them in what is now Belgium. The Romans set up military fortifications at the Chief Place of the Belgae, and the Roman word for those fortifications was **castra** – camps. When the Romans left in AD 410, the newly arrived Saxons called the city **Wintanceastre,** pronouncing **castra** as **'chester'.** There are many UK 'chesters', all of them once Roman fortifications. The Saxons didn't have a 'v' sound, so pronounced the Roman 'v' as 'w'; so **'Venta Castra'** became **'Winta-chester'**, and over many years has morphed into today's Winchester.

Buckler's Hard: a 'hard' is an area of shoreline sufficiently firm to give easy

Winchester Cathedral iStock

Bucklers Hard, famous for shipbuilding

Agamemnon, were built at Buckler's Hard. Although shipbuilding declined at Buckler's Hard in the 19th century, the tradition is not completely lost, and a company building motor yachts now occupies the Agamemnon Yard.

Alton means '**old town**'. Famous for hop picking and breweries, it also has a church, the scene of a heroic battle in 1643 when the Royalist Captain JOHN BOLLE took refuge with his men and refused to surrender. He was killed fighting in the pulpit; the damage caused by the gunshot can still be seen in the church door today.

access to boats. In the days when heavy items needed to be moved between the ship and shore, solid ground was important and there wasn't always a wharf available. Buckler's Hard developed as a double row of workers' cottages with a broad working area, or 'hard', between them that led down to the river. From the 17th century on most timber in Hampshire was reserved for the Navy, much of it going to Portsmouth and other naval dockyards. However, many British naval vessels, including several of ADMIRAL NELSON'S fleet, e.g. HMS

Gunshot in the door of St Lawrence Church
CREATIVE COMMONS

WALKS

IT'S TIME FOR SOME VIGOROUS EXERCISE!

WALK 1: WINCHESTER
THE HEART OF THE ANCIENT CAPITAL

Duration: 1 hour
Distance: 1 mile
(fairly flat, suitable for wheelchairs)
Start: Tourist Information Centre in the
Victorian Guildhall. Turn right towards King
Alfred's statue.

King Alfred's statue iStock

The High Street started life 2,500 years ago; it was the main thoroughfare for Roman, Saxon and medieval Winchester and claims to be the oldest street in any English city! Ahead is the mayor's official residence, Abbey House. Excavated remains of St Mary's Abbey, founded by Alfred's Queen, Ealhswith, in the early 10th century, can be seen along Abbey Passage to the right. With King Alfred the Great on your left, continue straight ahead to the river. The City Bridge is said to have first been built by St Swithun, the 9th-century bishop and patron saint of Winchester.

The City Bridge

Turn right and follow the river walk. To your right is a remnant of the original Roman town walls, built in the 3rd century AD. Continue to

Winchester College CREATIVE COMMONS

school in England. Continue to the main college gate and pass the Headmaster's House. The next building is where Jane Austen spent her last weeks; she died here and is buried in the cathedral.

At the end of College Street, turn right to face Kingsgate and the tiny church of St Swithun. Through the gateway, you come to the Close Wall. Turn right and go through Prior's Gate. On your right is the medieval Cheyney Court, where

Bishop's Residence

Wharf Mill and turn right to see the best-preserved part of the City Walls and the ruins of Wolvesey Castle. Proceed into College Street where you will see, on your right, the current Bishop's residence, built in 1684.

On your left is Winchester College, founded by William of Wykeham in 1382, the oldest continuously running

bishops met to hear legal cases. Passing the medieval stables on your right, now used as music rooms, you'll see the buildings of the Pilgrims' School. The oldest parts are two adjacent early 14th-century timber-framed halls, originally accommodation for pilgrims. Today, boys of the cathedral and college choirs -Choristers and Quiristers respectively- are educated here.

On your right are the massive columns marking the entrance to the former Chapter House. Turn left at the cathedral nave, walking beneath the flying buttresses. Turn past the west front of the Cathedral to the site of the Old Minster, dating from the 7th century. The New Minster was built on the instructions of Alfred the Great and completed by his son Edward the Elder. With the front of the Cathedral on your immediate right, follow the path directly ahead until you come to the pedestrian section of the High Street. Turn right to return to the Guildhall.

Winchester Cathedral Shutterstock/Richard Melichar

WALK 2: WINCHESTER
THE UPPER CITY

Duration: 1½ hours
Distance: Approximately 1 mile (some stairs and fairly steep slopes, generally unsuitable for wheelchairs)

Queen Anne statue

Start on the High Street on the corner of Market Lane and the 'new' Market Hall, built in 1772. Turn left into Market Lane and then right into The Square. Continue past the City Museum and turn right. In the 11th century, this area was part of the Royal Palace built by William the Conqueror. Coming back to the High Street you will see on your right the Butter Cross, dating from at least early 14th century.

Turn left into the High Street and continue ahead. The Town Clock and the statue of Queen Anne below were presented to the city in 1713, following a royal visit. They adorn the old Guildhall, where the city's curfew bell has hung since 1361, and is still rung each evening at 8pm. Continue up the High Street, crossing Southgate Street, passing the Horse and Rider statue (Elizabeth Frink, 1975) on your left. Straight ahead is Westgate, marking the line of the western city defences. A museum on the first floor houses the city's post-medieval

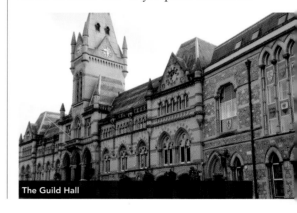
The Guild Hall

Horse sculpture

collection and historic weights and measures, with good views across Winchester from the roof.

Turn left up the pedestrian way next to the Westgate. You soon reach the excavated remains of Winchester Castle, begun by William the Conqueror in 1066.

Ahead is the 13th-century Great Hall, the only part of the medieval castle to survive above ground, and home to the famous Round Table. Go through the Great Hall and out into Queen Eleanor's Garden, a reconstruction of a medieval garden. The wall forming one side of the garden is all that remains in situ of The King's House built by Christopher Wren for Charles II in 1683. Go to the end of the garden, up the stairs, turn right and then left into the Winchester Military Museums complex; the large open square, now landscaped, was the parade ground of the Peninsula Barracks.

Steps to Westgate Museum

Round Table in the Great Hall CREATIVE COMMONS

Cross the square, keeping the former Sergeant's Mess (the building with the clock) on your left. Just past this, descend the steps to your left. This steep slope marks the eastern defences of the medieval castle. At the bottom of the steps turn left and then right, heading towards the spire of St Thomas's Church. Follow the driveway between Serles House and the church, passing the Guard House on your left. Cross Southgate Street, turn left and then right down the steps into 13th-century St Thomas Passage and at the end turn left into St Thomas Street. Cross the road and turn right into Minster Lane towards the cathedral. Take the diagonal path back towards Market Street and the High Street, noticing on your way the War Memorial at the front of the Cathedral.

Sergeant's Mess

War Memorial

GHOST STORIES

TERRIFYING TALES FROM HAUNTED HAMPSHIRE

BEAULIEU'S GHOSTLY BROTHERS

Monks dressed in brown habits are often seen at Beaulieu Abbey. The smell of incense drifts through the Palace House, and the sound of Gregorian chanting is sometimes heard before a death in the village. Beaulieu Manor, meanwhile, is said to have two ghosts, one a manservant who murdered a maid, and who can be seen at the top of the stairs in the Manor, and a Royalist soldier who was killed in a small room above a secret staircase.

GHOSTLY TROUBLES AT WINCHESTER THEATRE

Winchester's Theatre Royal is said to haunted by **John Simpkin** who, with his brother James, founded the theatre in 1913. James decided he would place only one set of initials above the stage, and engraved JS rather than J&JS, as his brother wanted him to do, in order that they could both be acknowledged. James thought the JS could refer to both of them.

Beaulieu Manor SHUTTERSTOCK/DAVE GREENBERG

John died before any changes could be made, and although James had promised he would add another J, he never did it before John died. John's ghost can sometimes be seen coming from his office and walking round the circle, stopping halfway and looking up to see if the initials have been changed before walking round to the opposite side of the circle.

What is now the prompt corner beside the stage used to be the place where the spotlight operator would sit during performances. One of the first shows staged at the theatre was a musical featuring dancing girls, among them the girlfriend of one of the spotlight operators. However, before the show began its run he was called up to fight in World War I. The girl was on stage one night when she briefly fainted; the manager, James Simpkin, came to her after the show to check that she was OK and she told him she'd seen her boyfriend in the prompt corner.

That very day, the spotlight operator's mother received a telegram to say her son had died in action. Not only can the spotlight operator still occasionally be seen today, but so can the dancing girl looking for her beloved.

THE HEADLESS LADY

The ghost of Dame Alice Lisle is said to haunt the Eclipse Inn and Moyles Court in Winchester. In 1685 Dame Alice sheltered two rebels from the Duke of Monmouth's defeated army at her house, Moyles Court, near Ringwood. When they were discovered, the old lady was sentenced to be dragged through the streets before being burnt at the stake. However, public outcry meant the sentence was reduced to decapitation, and she stepped out onto the scaffold from the window of the Eclipse Inn on 2 September 1685. She can still be seen at the Inn and around Moyles Court, but always with her head on her shoulders.

A HOST OF GHOSTS AT BRAMSHILL

Bramshill House, near Hazeley, now home to the National Police College, is also believed to be home to several ghosts.

The Grey Lady is the most commonly seen. She is usually spotted early in the morning and leaves the distinctive smell of lilies of the valley in her wake. The White Lady is said to be the ghost of a young bride who hid herself in the Mistletoe Bough chest that is in the reception area at Bramshill. She chose to hide in the chest during a Christmas game of hide-and-seek, fell asleep and suffocated. Some say this happened in Italy and that it's the ghost of Genevre Orsini, who died in 1727. The chest was brought back (with its ghost) to Bramshill.

A little green man, whom only children can see, is thought to be the

Ghostly lady iStock

ghost of the eccentric gardener and friend to George III, Henry Cope. He would only wear green clothes and eat green food, and his rooms, horses and carriages were also decorated in green.

Other reported ghosts inlcude a deer keeper who was accidentally shot by an archbishop; a nun and a woman in Stuart-style clothes in the chapel; a man with a long beard; and a tennis player from the 1930s, said to be the son of Lord Brocket, the last private owner of Bramshill, who died after falling from a train at Surbiton.

SHUTTERSTOCK/ANKI HOGLUND

THE GHOSTLY SOUNDS OF BATTLE

During the Civil War, the colonel of the Royalists was besieged in Alton's St Lawrence's Church and made an heroic stand in battle. He fought bravely and killed many Roundheads before he was killed himself. Sometimes the haunting sounds of the battle's re-enactment can be heard throughout the church, although nothing has ever been seen.

THE NEW FOREST'S GHOSTLY KING

When William the Conqueror died, he left the throne to his younger son, who became William II. His older brother was furious and organised a revolt, supported by many of the Norman landowners who'd been given their estates through the generosity of his father. When William II found out what was going on, he cannily quashed the danger by promising the

St Lawrence's Church, Alton CREATIVE COMMONS

native Anglo-Saxons massive reforms in taxes and restrictive laws. However, the minute the threats disappeared his pledges were abandoned! In fact, he raised taxes and made the laws even more harsh.

With all this in mind, it's no wonder that when he arrived in the New Forest in the year 1100, for a few days' hunting, an 'accident' occurred, resulting in the death of this hated king. He was found with an arrow in his chest. The arrow belonged to Sir William Tyrrel, one of the hunting party; he claimed it was a dreadful mistake and disappeared to France. William was so unpopular that all his companions ran off to secure their estates against the expected retribution for the king's death, and abandoned his body where it lay. A local charcoal worker found it, put it in his cart and took it to Winchester to be buried.

Along the route a trail of royal blood was left as it dripped from the body. This forest 'blood-trail' is reputed to still lie there, and the king's ghost can sometimes be seen retracing his last journey. A memorial called the Rufus Stone (the King was nicknamed Rufus because of his red face) was erected to mark the spot where he died; this is where his ghost occasionally restarts his last journey.

The Rufus Stone marks the spot where King William lost his life

'WOO' WATERLOOVILLE

Hopfield House in Waterlooville, near Portsmouth, was built in the 19th century by Edward Fawkes, a self-made businessman who, like lots of prosperous Victorians, wanted a house that would reflect his wealth and provide a good inheritance for future generations. Fawkes declared that the house should always remain in his family. However, his grandson, who eventually inherited it, found it too large, and rented it out. The first tenants were a childless couple of spiritualists. They claimed that Fawkes' ghost came to them, threatening all manner of terrors if they refused to move out. They moved!

They sub-let it to a widow and her adult daughter. The daughter found her mother dead in bed one morning, with a horror-struck face, and so moved out herself. The Fawkes family had had enough by this time and sold Hopfield House to a retired army captain and his wife. One day the captain was found dead in the hallway, stabbed in the back with one of his own Indian daggers. No culprit was ever found and his widow quickly moved out.

The next owners were the Daltons, who bought it in the 1920s. One of the daughters reported that she hated the house from the first moment she set eyes on it, and sensed an evil atmosphere. Once she felt something invisible heavily hit her head and another time woke up to find herself under the bed, with no explanation. Her brother, a popular and clever student at Oxford, for no apparent reason shot himself in the basement; his mother didn't recover from the shock and died shortly after.

Eventually, Hampshire County Council bought the house and turned it into flats. There are still rumours of strange happenings and ghostly figures at windows today . . .

THE GHOSTS OF WARBLINGTON

The headless ghost of Margaret Pole, Countess of Salisbury, is rumoured to haunt the ruins of Warblington Castle, which Henry VIII gave to her

iStock

Elsewhere in Warblington, the Old Rectory in Pook Lane (once called Spook Lane), on the site of the parsonage, is home to a whistling ghost. He is thought to be an evil former parson who had fathered a number of illegitimate children by his maid and then murdered them.

THE SPIRITS OF CRONDALL

There is an avenue of trees leading to All Saints' Church in Crondall, that is said to be haunted by two ghosts: a man on horseback wearing armour, and a foot-soldier in thigh boots and breastplate who walks into the church, kneels down at the altar and then disappears. Nearby Alma Lane is also thought to be haunted, with the sound of running footsteps belonging to a military messenger. He was murdered while carrying the news of the victory at Waterloo from Portsmouth to Aldershot.

in 1513, and the churchyard. Henry subsequently had her put to death for treason in the Tower of London. It was said that the executioner was young and inexperienced and made a complete mess of the beheading, which was a long drawn-out affair.

LOCAL EVENTS

OUT AND ABOUT IN HAMPSHIRE

FARNBOROUGH AIRSHOW

Farnborough International Airshow is a week-long event held in mid-July in even-numbered years at Farnborough Airport. The first five days (Monday to Friday) are dedicated exclusively to trade, with the final two days open to the public. It's the largest airshow in Europe, attracting hundreds of thousands of visitors.

A Boeing Super Constellation comes in to land

> *"Once you have tasted flight, you will forever walk the earth with your eyes turned skyward"*
>
> Leonardo da Vinci

The airshow is an important event in the international aerospace and defence industry calendar, providing an opportunity to demonstrate civilian and military aircraft to potential customers and investors.

Typhoon taking off TIM HORNE

The show is also used for the announcement of new developments and orders, and to attract media coverage.

The airshow originated from the annual RAF Airshow at Hendon in 1920 and in 1948 moved to its present location of Farnborough, home of the Royal Aircraft Establishment, about 30 miles south-west of central London. In 1952, 31 people were killed (29 spectators, one pilot and a navigator) when a de Havilland DH.110 jet fighter disintegrated in flight and crashed into the crowd. At the 1958 show, the RAF Black Arrows executed a 22-plane formation loop, a world record which remains unbroken to this day.

Billions of dollars of orders are taken – the recent show (my ears are still ringing from Typhoon Eurofighters!) estimates a huge $201 billion worth. However, it's not just about big business; it also provides an opportunity to showcase the UK's proud heritage in aviation, and people still watch spellbound at the stunning display the Red Arrows put on; and of course the show always finishes with that most lovable of British planes, the mighty Spitfire.

ISLE OF WIGHT FESTIVAL

Slightly more peaceful (but not necessarily any quieter!) is the famous Isle of Wight Festival, which takes place every June in Newport on the Isle of Wight, just a few miles off the south coast of Hampshire. It's steeped in history and recognised around the world for its great line-ups, mixing top-name artists with the hottest 'hip and happening' acts! The Festival is famed for its heritage and is the UK's first major music event of the summer festival season. The original Isle of Wight Festival took place at the end of the 1960s during the 'summer of love'.

Isle of Wight Festival CREATIVE COMMONS

A series of legendary events then featured performances from Bob Dylan, The Who, Free, The Doors, Joni Mitchell, Jefferson Airplane and many more. In 1970, 600,000 hippies descended on the island to see Jimi Hendrix perform his penultimate concert. The Festival marked a turning point in UK music history and played a major role in shaping the music festivals we know today. In 2002, the Isle of Wight Festival was reincarnated following a 32-year gap.

Since its rebirth the Festival has seen headline performances from some of the biggest acts in the world, including The Rolling Stones, Bruce Springsteen and The E Street Band, Paul McCartney, Pearl Jam, Kasabian, Jay-Z, The Strokes, The Who, David Bowie and Coldplay, amongst others.

Summer of Love iStock

LETS GO FLY A KITE!

The Portsmouth International Kite Festival has taken place in August for nearly a quarter of a century. Spread over three days at Southsea Common, Portsmouth, it's recognised as one of the best kite festivals in the world. The 2014 event hosted kite fliers from as far afield as Singapore, Japan, America and New Zealand, as well as European and British kite lovers, of course.

Kite Festival iStock

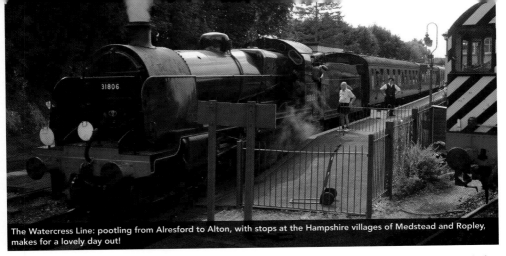

The Watercress Line: pootling from Alresford to Alton, with stops at the Hampshire villages of Medstead and Ropley, makes for a lovely day out!

Guest fliers put on colourful demonstrations of kites, including swarms of snakes, frogs, lizards, whales, jesters, fish, salamanders and much more. Visitors can also see beautiful single-line kites, intricately appliquéd or painted with magnificent designs; amazing cellular kites – flying miracles of structural engineering – awe-inspiring 3D soft kites in a magical range of shapes and sizes, and skilfully flown kites performing excellent tricks and routines to music! Many of these expert kite fliers have been coming to the kite festival for years.

THE WATERCRESS LINE

Watercress used to be sent by stagecoach from farms in Arlesford to London but later it went by rail on a line that became known as the Watercress Line. The Watercress Line steam railway still exists and is a major tourist attraction in Hampshire. It now carries tourists (rather than the salad crop!) the short distance from Alresford to Alton.

LOCAL SPORTS

SAILING

Relatively safe waters mean Hampshire has developed into one of the busiest sailing areas in the country, with many yacht clubs and several manufacturers on the Solent. The Round Island Boat Race, which takes place at Cowes on the Isle of Wight for a week in June every year, attracts huge international crowds, both participants and spectators.

The race is a real test of skill; for the 2014 edition, lack of wind saw competitors 'becalmed' for long periods of the day. A huge 669 boats had to retire but there were still 724 recorded finishers! As well as sailing, the sport of windsurfing was invented at Hayling Island, located the south-east of the county.

Cowes week, Isle of Wight CREATIVE COMMONS

CRICKET

The Bat and Ball at Hambledon is regarded as the birthplace of English cricket, with one of the first teams forming there in 1750; the Hambledon Club created many of cricket's early rules. The founder of Lord's Cricket Ground, **Sir Thomas Lord**, is buried at nearby West Meon.

The Rose Bowl: home of Hampshire Cricket Club CREATIVE COMMONS

The Bat and Ball at Hambledon

Today, Hampshire County Cricket Club is a successful first-class team. The main county ground is the Rose Bowl in West End, Southampton, which has hosted several one-day internationals and which, following redevelopment, hosted its first test match in 2011. Notable players include ex-England batsman **Kevin Pietersen**. Hampshire has also been captained by the famous Australian leg-spinner, **Shane Warne**.

FOOTBALL

Hampshire has several notable association football teams: **Southampton FC** (known as *'The Saints'*) is currently in the Premier League, while **Portsmouth FC** (nicknamed *'Pompey'*) is in League Two. The Saints and Pompey have traditionally been fierce rivals.

Portsmouth won the FA Cup in 1939 and 2008 and the Football League title twice, in 1949 and 1950, but have spent much of the last 50 years outside the top division, including several seasons in the Fourth Division; they are currently competing once again in the lowest division in senior football. Southampton, meanwhile, won the FA Cup in 1976, reached the final in 2003 and spent 27 unbroken years in England's top division between 1978 and 2005 before making a successful return to the top flight in 2012.

Conference Premier side Aldershot FC became members of the Football League in 1932 but never progressed beyond the Third Division, and on 25 March 1992 went into liquidation and were forced to resign from the league. A new football club, Aldershot Town FC (*'The Shots'*) was formed almost immediately, and started life in Division 3 of the Isthmian League. In 2008, after several exceptional seasons, Aldershot Town were crowned the Conference Premier champions and were promoted into the Football League. Sadly – and I say this as they're my nearest local team – they subsequently spiralled rapidly downhill and fell back out of the league five years later. Their fans never give up hope, though, and I'm sure, as Arnie would say, *'they'll be back'* . . .

MOTOR SPORTS

Thruxton Circuit, in the north of the county, is Hampshire's top motor racing circuit. Like many race circuits Thruxton was originally a wartime airfield. Commissioned in 1941, the airfield was host to both the RAF and USAF and played a major part in the D-Day landings as a base for troop-carrying aircraft and gliders.

Thruxton Racing Circuit SHUTTERSTOCK/STEVE MANN

After the war, motorsport started in 1950 with motor bikes on a track made up of runways and perimeter roads. Cars joined the bikes in 1952. However, the deteriorating wartime tarmac was breaking up badly and in 1968 a new track opened, including lots of tight corners! Thruxton has seen nearly all our recent Formula 1 drivers race regularly at the track at some time in their career. In 1993 Damon Hill, Formula 1 World Champion, drove a demonstration run in the Williams FW15C, recording an incredible 57.6-second lap of the 2.4-mile circuit, an average speed of 147.25mph.

It's now the high speed rounds of the British Touring Car championship and Superbikes that regularly bring in capacity crowds. If you follow these series you may have seen Thruxton on the TV – or even lapped the circuit on the PlayStation Touring Car game!

Still on the theme of cars, you can find the National Motor Museum in the New Forest adjacent to Beaulieu Palace House. Housing a collection of over 250 cars and motorbikes, the museum tells the story of motoring on Britain's roads from the dawn of motoring to the present day; you can see world land speed record breakers, including the Campbells' famous Bluebirds, and film favourites such as the magical flying car, Chitty Chitty Bang Bang.

Donald Campbell's famous Bluebird, at National Motor Museum

LOCAL HISTORY

THE VERY OLD STUFF!

Hampshire takes its name from the original settlement that's now the city of Southampton. Southampton was known in Old English as Hamtun, loosely meaning 'village-town', so its surrounding area (its scir) became known as Hamtunscir. In the Domesday Book the old name was mis-recorded as Hantescire, so that's where the modern abbreviation 'Hants' comes from!

When the Romans invaded Britain in AD 43 (for the second time – very persistent, those Romans), Hampshire was quickly, and apparently peacefully, incorporated into the Roman province of Britannia. Venta (Winchester) became the capital of most of Hampshire and Wiltshire, as far west as Bath. For most of the next three centuries, southern Britain enjoyed relative peace. The Romans officially withdrew from Britain in AD 410 and Hampshire eventually emerged as the centre of what was to become the most powerful kingdom in Britain, the Kingdom of Wessex.

A statue in Winchester celebrates the powerful **King Alfred**, who fought off the Vikings and brought peace to the region in the 9th century. He was also a great scholar, who commissioned the Anglo-Saxon Chronicle, a powerful tool in the development of our English identity. **King Alfred** proclaimed himself 'King of England' in 886, but it wasn't until 927 that he officially controlled the whole of England.

King Alfred iSTOCK

A BIT LATER ON!

By the time of the Norman Conquest, Winchester had been overtaken by London as the largest city in England, and after this time **King William I** made it his capital. The centre of political power moved away from Hampshire, although Winchester remained important, mainly because having the New Forest close by provided prized royal hunting grounds!

From the 12th century, the coastal ports grew in importance, fuelled by trade with the continent, wool and cloth manufacture – which Hampshire did very well – and the fishing industry (lots of rivers and the sea, of course), and a shipbuilding industry was established. This was made even more convenient by the abundant local supply of oak from the nearby New Forest. (By the way, Hampshire is the third most densely wooded county in England.) By 1523, the population of Southampton had overtaken that of Winchester.

Over several centuries, a series of castles and forts were built along the coast of the Solent to defend the harbours at Southampton and Portsmouth. These include the Roman Portchester Castle, which overlooks Portsmouth Harbour, and a series of forts built by Henry VIII, including Hurst Castle, situated on a sand spit at the mouth of the Solent, Calshot Castle on another spit at the mouth of Southampton Water, and Netley Castle.

CAN A WAR EVER BE 'CIVIL'?!

No county was more affected by the Civil War than Hampshire, where Cromwell finally closed in on Charles I, first in 1644 at the Battle of Cheriton and then in 1645 at Basing House. Cromwell decided enough was enough and it was time to mop up in the south, and where better to

Basing House gate CREATIVE COMMONS

Calshot Castle SHUTTERSTOCK/HELEN HOTSON

begin than Basing House, a garrison that had defied him for two long years. He marched on Basing from Winchester, accompanied by 7,000 troops! The Royalist Catholic garrison refused to surrender and a quarter of its inhabitants were killed, including six priests, and the house was burned to the ground.

THE SEA, THE SEA . . .

Portsmouth and Southampton remained important harbours when others, like Poole and Bristol, declined – they're two of only a very few locations that combine deep water with shelter. Southampton has been host to many famous ships, including the Mayflower and the Titanic. In fact, three-quarters of Titanic's crew came from the city, many working as stokers in the ship's engine rooms or as stewards looking after passengers. When Titanic set off from Southampton docks on its maiden voyage to New York on 10 April 1912,

the people cheered it off with pride. Five days later, when the liner hit an iceberg and sank in the North Atlantic, Southampton was plunged into mourning and many of the victims' families were left in poverty.

THE MILITARY

Hampshire played a crucial role in World War II due to the large Royal Navy harbour at Portsmouth, the army camp at Aldershot, and Netley military hospital near Southampton. Spitfire designers, Supermarine, were based in Southampton, which is one of the reasons the city took such a severe bombing.

Aldershot is renowned as the 'home of the British Army' and nearby Farnborough is a major centre for the aviation industry; in October 1908 Samuel Cody made the first aeroplane flight in Britain from here, and two of Farnborough's historic wind tunnels are now listed buildings. The first was built in 1917 and the other, much larger, in 1935 and was used extensively for research into Concorde's aerodynamics, as well as by Formula 1 cars, until its closure in the early 1990s. Sir Frank Whittle conducted much of his research into jet aircraft here, and a replica of the Gloster E.28/39 (based on his prototype) stands on a roundabout in the town as tribute to its inventor.

Frank Whittle's Gloster CREATIVE COMMONS

M3 - Twyford Down cutting CREATIVE COMMONS

A MODERN-DAY BATTLE!

We spoke earlier about battles, and there's one more that deserves a mention here: the Battle of Twyford Down. In 1990 the M3 motorway was still unfinished and to complete it there would have to be a tunnel or a cutting through Twyford Down, just outside Winchester. The tunnel would have cost the government £75 million more than the cutting, so you can guess which option won the day!

However, 'the natives were revolting' and in December 1991 Twyford Down became the site of the UK's first road protest camp. A year later the first camp was evicted but a new one attracted even more public support (sometimes over 5,000 people) and obstructed the work. However, the battle was eventually lost and in 1994 the final link completing the M3 was opened, with 4.7 acres of Twyford Down lost.

FAMOUS LOCALS

THEY LOOK VERY FAMILIAR...

Famous Victorian novelist, journalist, and social commentator, **Charles Dickens** (*David Copperfield*, *Nicholas Nickleby* and many, many more) was born in Portsmouth on 7 February 1812 in Old Commercial Road. It was a comfortable home, but Charles was forced to leave school at a relatively early age to work in a factory when his father was thrown into debtors' prison.

There's a touching tale relating that, at the height of his fame, Charles wandered Portsmouth's smoky streets looking in vain for the house where he'd been born (he'd been back twice before, to research locations for *Nicholas Nickleby*, and to give readings). He probably wouldn't have any trouble today as the house has been turned into a museum and is well signposted!

A Christmas Carol by Charles Dickens CREATIVE COMMONS

Another very famous British author, **Jane Austen**, was born in Steventon in the north-east of the county in 1775, and spent her first 25 years there. She was the seventh child and second daughter of the rector, **Revd George Austen**, and his wife, **Cassandra**. Two of her brothers became clergymen, one inherited rich estates, and two became admirals in the Royal Navy; like her sister, Jane never married. She spent some time in Canterbury and Bath, but after her father died, moved with

Jane Austen's house at Chawton AUTHOR

Jane Austen CREATIVE COMMONS

her sister and mother to Southampton and then to Chawton, where she stayed for eight years and wrote most of her novels. These include *Pride and Prejudice* (made world famous by the TV production which starred Colin

Firth as the austere but attractive Mr Darcy), *Emma, Mansfield Park, Sense and Sensibility, Persuasion* and *Northanger Abbey*. Jane was a very astute social observer, and the fact that so many of her books have been adapted as films or TV drama series is testament to their enduring popularity.

She became ill in 1816, and in 1817 her family took her to Winchester for medical treatment. Unfortunately, the doctors could do nothing for her and she died there, aged only 41; she was buried in the north aisle of Winchester Cathedral.

Clifton Suspension Bridge in Bristol SHUTTERSTOCK/JON LE-BON

The great engineer, **Isambard Kingdom Brunel,** was born in Portsmouth in 1806. He built 25 railway lines and over 100 bridges, including the magnificent Clifton Suspension Bridge in Bristol, as well as piers, dock systems, and ships.

> *"I do always look towards Hampshire and plan my return. I'm sure it'll happen one day."*

Colin Firth as Mr Darcy in Jane Austen's Pride and Prejudice. Incidentally, Colin is also a Hampshire lad!

The Reverend Gilbert White was a pioneering 18th-century naturalist who lived and worked in the charming Hampshire village of Selborne. He believed in studying living birds and animals in their natural habitat, which was an unusual approach at that time, as most naturalists preferred

Gilbert White's house and gardens at Selborne JOHN ELDER

to carry out detailed examinations of dead specimens in the comfort of their studios. White was the first to distinguish the chiffchaff, willow warbler and wood warbler as three separate species, largely due to their different songs, and he was the first to accurately describe the harvest mouse and the noctule bat. His world-famous book *The Natural History of Selborne* was published in 1789, just four years before his death. It is reputed to be the fourth most published book in the English language and has never been out of print.

His house, set in 25 acres of restored gardens and ancient parkland, is now a fascinating museum dedicated to his work, as well as that of Antarctic hero **Captain Lawrence Oates**, who travelled the epic journey of discovery to the South Pole in 1911–12 with **Captain Scott**.

Pre-Raphaelite painter, **Sir John Everett Millais**, was born in Southampton and has a gallery in the town named after him. Other well-known people born in Southampton include comedian **Benny Hill**, film director **Ken Russell**, singer/songwriter **Howard Jones** and TV gardener **Charlie Dimmock**.

Sherlock Holmes iSTOCK

Sherlock Holmes author (and one-time Portsmouth FC goalkeeper!) **Sir Arthur Conan Doyle** and former Prime Minister **James Callaghan** were both born in Portsmouth. Speaking of Sherlock Holmes, the

Dr Watson, I presume! **Martin Freeman** and **Benedict Cumberbatch** CREATIVE COMMONS

most recent actor to play Dr Watson, sidekick to super-sleuth Holmes, is **Martin Freeman**, who was born in Aldershot. Martin first came to public attention for his role as Tim in The Office, alongside **Ricky Gervais** and **Mackenzie Crook**. He went on to play Bilbo Baggins in the recent *Hobbit* films, as well as a recent TV adaptation of the Coen Brothers' wonderful black comedy, *Fargo*.

Nicholas Lyndhurst, of Only Fools and Horses fame, was born in

Emsworth, and **John Arlott**, the famous voice of cricket, was, as the title of his autobiography tells us, a Basingstoke Boy.

Not born but buried in Hampshire is **Napoleon III**. Farnborough is a pretty unlikely place for the end of the Napoleonic dynasty! With his wife, **Princess Eugenie**, Napoleon III fled to England in 1870 after the disastrous Franco-Prussian war. Three years later the Emperor died and his widow moved to Farnborough and acquired Farnborough Hill. In 1887 she built a huge mausoleum.

In a vaulted crypt there are three impressive granite sarcophagi, one each for the Emperor, their son the Prince Imperial, who died fighting British troops in the Zulu war, and one for herself. She died in 1920 aged 94. She also established St Michael's Abbey at the same location, which today is still run by Benedictine monks.

Bibliography

BALDOCK, DOROTHY, *A Taste of Hampshire and Wiltshire,* 1995, J. Salmon

Collected Memories of Hampshire: Personal Memories inspired by the Francis Frith Collection, 2013, THE FRANCIS FRITH COLLECTION

The Complete Atlas of the British Isles, 1965, The Reader's Digest Association

HINTON, DAVID and DR A.N. NOBLE, *Hampshire and the Isle of Wight,* 1988, George Philip/Ordnance Survey

LEGG, PENNY, *Haunted Southampton,* 2011, The History Press

RANCE, ADRIAN, *Shire County Guide: Hampshire,* 1988, Shire Publications Ltd

VAN DER KISTE, JOHN, *A Grim Almanac of Hampshire,* 2011, The History Press

WILSON, SIR JAMES, KCSI, *The Dialect of the New Forest in Hampshire,* 1913, Oxford University Press

WINN, CHRISTOPHER, *I Never Knew That About England,* 2005, Random House

WOOD, ROBERT, *Walks into History,* 2009, Countryside Books

www3.hants.gov.uk/austen/deane-parsonage.htm (accessed June 2014)

www.southernlife.org.uk/villinde.htm (accessed June 2014)

www.visitwinchester.co.uk/sites/default/files/City%20Walk.pdf (accessed July 2014)

www.insidehampshire.co.uk/food-and-drink/ (accessed June 2014)

http://en.wikipedia.org/w/index.php?title=English_in_southern_England#Hampshire (accessed July 2014)

www.westerngazette.co.uk/900-years-ago-hated-King-murder-Royal-Ghost/story-20479157-detail/story.html (accessed June 2014)

www.charlesdickensbirthplace.co.uk (accessed July 2014)